Contents

GW00802244

First published in Great Britain in 2008 byPenhaligon's Friends
© Copyright Penhaligon's Friends

© Compiled by Reverend Mike Kippax, Reverend Dr Peter Johnson, Wendy Ball & Alice Allsworth
© Illustrations & Design by Jenny Nightingale   www.jennynightingale.co.uk

Introduction

Why this book is needed

The involvement of the Christian church in the lives of the bereaved comes at one of the most vulnerable times in anyone's existence. Raw grief and outward expressions of those emotions can be overwhelming and leave the comforters feeling ill- equipped to deal with the family's grief journey. Not only that but all family members may grieve differently and need varying kinds of support and understanding at different times. Out of the ashes of mourning new life is possible, restoration and reconstitution can become a reality.

Who this book is intended for

All those who are involved from the earliest contact to the ongoing pastoral care of bereaved families need to feel equipped to deal with what surfaces and to know where to turn for other help when necessary. The aim of this book is to enhance and inform existing skills and develop new ones for all those caring for bereaved families, in particular their children. This book focuses on the needs of bereaved children and how they can be helped to grieve healthily.

How it can help

For some children and families spirituality is inseparable from religious faith, for others it is outside a religious context. It is important to understand a child's spiritual background and beliefs as this helps the professional demonstrate respect for and interest in every aspect of their lives. Opportunities to fulfil religious customs can be of deep importance to some families. We need to listen carefully to children's descriptions of their thoughts, feelings and understanding of their faith so that the children feel heard and supported.

Biblical Contexts

Jesus himself was a "man of sorrows and acquainted with grief" He felt the range of human emotions upon the death of His friend Lazarus. He proclaimed Himself as one who would bestow a garment of praise instead of the ashes of mourning; He would tell those who mourned that the time of God's favour had come. Jesus promised not to leave His disciples comfortless when He explained they would have another comforter.

As Christians we are commanded to care for the orphans and the widows, to weep with those who weep and to comfort those who mourn. Given the raw emotion of human grief it is easy to feel overwhelmed at times and unable to share that grief journey with a family. There are moments when the bereft will have big and awkward questions to which we don't have the answer, when we may be unsure of what to say or do.

Adults have a larger vocabulary to express those feelings if they choose to. Children often do not and they will show their feelings in their behaviour. Accepting that we cannot 'fix' anyone's grief, only support them through it, can lessen the feelings of helplessness.

foreword

Excitedly, we piled into our car – mum in the driving seat, dad by her side, me on his lap and my newly-born brother behind us in his carry-cot. Our plan: to be in Nottingham by teatime. East of Okehampton, mum lost control of the car. By teatime she was dead.

Friends and family were sympathetic but dad didn't want to talk much about it. Someone decided that a funeral service was no place for an eight year old. My school report that term simply recorded, "Michael has been handicapped by long periods away from school."

These were the 1950's, when adults still remembered the horrors of war. You quickly learned to 'put up and shut up'; to be a man! At the time, I thought I was coping rather well, but within two years my class position had fallen from 'high' to 'medium' and then to 'low'.
    "I hope he will try harder next term." wrote my headmaster.

How would you cope with a grieving child like me? In these more enlightened days, what comfort and counsel would you offer? There are no easy answers, but this book will prove an invaluable guide. I commend it to you wholeheartedly.

Reverend Mike Kippax

Understanding Children's
Spiritual Development

"When we talk about facilitating the spiritual formation of children,
we need to remember that through the various stages of childhood,
children relate to God and understand God in ways
that are different from those of adults."
(Beckwith pg 41)

Research has shown that spiritual development begins and is settled
early in life.

* A person's moral foundations are generally in place by the
time they reach the age of nine
* What someone believes about God at age 13 is what they are
most likely to hold onto for the rest of their life
* A person's response to the meaning and personal value of
Jesus' life, death and resurrection is usually determined
before age 18

Children want to know who made the world and everything in it and
how they can relate to the Creator. This simple need isn't based on
their mental ability, knowledge or depth of understanding but their
innate curiosity about the world around them. Adults often make the
assumption that children think like them but don't feel like them.
Studies conducted by Jean Piaget showed that the reverse is true, that
children have to develop thinking processes before they begin to think
like adults.

James Fowler suggests that a child's spiritual understanding is closely
linked to their mental and emotional development and they pass
through distinct stages in developing their spirituality at their own pace.

Research has shown that young children will believe in God or a supreme being even when an adult has told them there is no God. How they think about God is fired by their imagination not logic.

Pre-school Children

* Their picture of God is influenced by their parents, and they need help to make Him real.
* They may see God as the ideal parent, all powerful and all knowing, responding to Him because they are usually so much smaller than everything else in their world.

Primary School Children

* They are losing their self-centred view of the world and understand God more in the context of one who keeps score of good and bad behaviour.
* Their literal and concrete thinking enables them to understand that the world is made up of many different people with different ideas and abilities.
* They can have a strong belief in a God who has human characteristics. It is natural for them to think of God as loving, kind, caring and real, someone they can know and trust.

As children grow and develop their spiritual understanding they should be encouraged to question and work through what they don't understand. By taking their questions seriously and giving them information relevant to their age they will feel valued and encouraged to talk about even the more difficult things.

How Children Grieve

How children experience and react to death may be different from an adult. One of the differences is that intense emotion and behavioural expression are not continuous in children.

A child's grief may appear to be more intermittent and brief than adults but in fact usually lasts longer. (Worden, J .1996)

Adults could be said to wade through rivers of grief, for children their grief is more like jumping in and out of puddles.

Many parents and carers find this movement in and out of grief hard to deal with or understand. It can be wrongly assumed that because a child is playing happily they are coping well with the bereavement. In fact they may be hiding many feelings and seek to play or become easily distracted because they find staying in the intensity of grief intolerable.

Children's Responses to Grief

How a child responds to grief is influenced by many factors such as the type of death, the relationship to the dead person, the grieving process of their carer and the age of the child. There is a wide variation in how children grieve when someone has died.

The reactions can be:
* Shock and disbelief
* Dismay and protest
* Apathy and being stunned
* Continuation of normal activities
(Dyregrov.A.1990)

Children's concepts of death change as they develop and their understanding about death and dying increases with age. Broadly speaking, it follows these patterns:

Infants
No understanding of death
Absorb emotion of those around them

Age 2-3 Years
Often confuse death with sleep
May exhibit loss of speech
(Wass H. Corr C 1984)

7

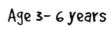

Age 3- 6 years

* This is the age of
magical thinking. Children
may believe their actions and
words caused the death or they can
bring the dead person back
* Do not always have the words to express feelings
* May exhibit disturbances in eating, sleep and
bladder control   (Grollman.E.A EA 1990)

Age 6-9 years

* Beginning to understand the finality of death
* Afraid that death is contagious and worried about who else is going to die
* May ask questions over and over again
* Often protect adults
* Usually very curious about death
* May have a strong sense of abandonment (Wass H. Corr C 1984)

Age 9-12 years

* View death as inevitable
* Understanding is nearer to adults
* Beginning to understand the finality of death
* Aware of the impact that the death will have on them

Age 13-18 years

* Understand the finality and universality of death (Grollman.E.A 1990)
* More interested in talking to peers than their family
* Death often viewed as the enemy

8

Tasks of Grief

William Worden (1991) suggests that grief is an essential and painful healing process, which is achieved through a series of tasks:

* Facing reality
* Experiencing the pain of grief
* Adjusting to the new reality
* Re-investing in the future and moving on with life

These tasks may be repeated in various ways at different times and the whole process may take a more roundabout route than previously assumed.

Some children may not be able to acknowledge what has happened and may cope by denying it at first. It is really important to give children the choice to see the dead person. Include them as much as possible in preparation and attendance at the funeral. This will help them face the reality of what has happened and begin to work through the process above.

Helping families Cope With
Serious Illness

Serious illness within the family can disrupt family life causing emotional, social and financial difficulties.

When someone is seriously ill, children need:

* To be given information a bit at a time
* To have information repeated in words they can understand
* To be involved in the care of the ill person (if they would like to be)
* To hear words such as cancer and death used when appropriate (Adults need to check that the child understands these words). Avoid euphemisms such as "big C" for cancer
* To be allowed to ask questions and have them answered honestly
* To be told what is going to happen.

"If I knew what
was happening
I would have said
goodbye"
Jane, 5

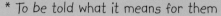

* To be told what it means for them
* To know who will be around to help them
* To express feelings, in words, play and art
* To be given an opportunity to express their anxieties
  and to receive reassurance where appropriate
* To be allowed to say good-bye
* To spend quality time with their family
* To play and have fun
* To have a routine

"only indeed, when he is given true information,
and the sympathy and support to bear it,
can a child or adolescent be expected to
respond to his loss with any degree of realism."
(Bowlby 1980)

Remember:
* Share your own feelings openly with the child
* The school or early years setting should be informed so they can
  support the child too.
* Don't be afraid to say "I don't know"
* Try not to make promises that you may not be able to keep.

Telling a Child Someone Has Died by Suicide

There are often complex circumstances surrounding a suicide. It is helpful to spend more time with the family to explore their feelings about their relationships before the death and their response to these events. Taking the time to do this is usually very therapeutic for the adults. Afterwards the adults are usually empowered and less afraid to talk to their children openly.

When someone has died through suicide the process of breaking bad news is the same as any death. It is just as important in these circumstances to be honest with the children and tell them that their special person has died - followed by **how** they died.

This can be done in stages and does not have to happen all in one go If children are not told that someone has died through suicide they may hear from others and not be able to discuss their feelings openly. Children cope better when they know the truth even though it is often difficult to tell them. Clergy can offer support and be around when the news is broken or be available to follow up and answer questions later if necessary. Pastoral workers need to take care of themselves at these times and may need to talk about their feelings concerning the situation The bereaved family may raise questions about suicide and faith.

"A child can live through anything so long as he or she is told the truth and is allowed to share the natural feelings people have when they are suffering"
(Eda Le Shan 1987)

Suicide Resource:

Winston's Wish provides a helpful booklet "Beyond the Rough Rocks" which can assist adults when telling children how the person died.
ISBN: 0-09539123-3-7

Traumatic Death

Following: Accidents, Suicide, Sudden Infant Death, Murder.

Children will often need to talk about the traumatic event before they can deal with the bereavement itself, particularly if they have been involved in the event. Although the family may want to protect the child from the facts this is an area when honesty may be more helpful. Common Reactions to Traumatic Grief:

FEELINGS

* Intense shock, with recurring images of the death even if not witnessed
* Sense of rejection or abandonment following suicide
* Irritable easily aroused by threat or upheaval, expressing extreme, unfocused rage
* Feeling guilty for surviving
* Anxious and pre-occupied by the trauma, specifically about threats of similar danger
* Blaming God, disbelief, loss of faith
* Withdrawal and avoidance of feelings

RESPONSES

* Avoiding objects, places and events that are associated with the event
* Heightened awareness to threat and danger
* Difficulties retaining pleasant memories- replaced by intrusive pictures or fantasies of the event
* Prolonged search for a reason or explanation of the tragedy
* Problems with sleeping including nightmares
* Different pattern of church attendance

RELATIONSHIPS

* Strained family relationships - often resulting in blame
* Stigma and isolation from the community

This group of children is more at risk of prolonged or unresolved grief.

14

Ideas to Help Children
Say Goodbye

At what age should children attend a funeral?

If parents are making a decision about whether a child should
attend a funeral or memorial service, age is not the most important
consideration. A child is part of the family and children who are old
enough to love are old enough to grieve. No child is too young to view a
body or attend a funeral, provided that they have been prepared and
lovingly guided through the process of what will happen and the things
they will see. Rather, if children are excluded they may think that death
and grief are too horrible to be faced and can feel alone.

Children need to learn that special, loved people do die. Children need
to be reassured that there will always be somebody to take care of
them.

Give the child the choice and include them whenever possible with activities such as:

* Choosing the coffin
* Placing a note,
  drawing, special
  object or memento
  in the coffin
* Picking special
  songs, music,
  readings

Ideas to Help Children
Say Goodbye (continued)

Where's
Molly Now?
A handbook for
Childhood Bereavement

Preparing children for viewing the body and attending the funeral

Viewing the body:

If the funeral director provides such a service parents can ask for a special viewing for children. They are often happy to explain to children what happens before and after a funeral. Parents should take children to visit the mortuary, chapel of rest or church ahead of time if possible. They can tell them that they don't have to stay there the whole time if they don't want to and can go outside with an adult to play or go for a walk.

Essentially parents can help their children understand:
* What **death** is.
* That the **funeral director** will go to the hospital or home to pick up the body.
* That the body is taken to the chapel of rest to be kept until it is buried or cremated.
* How the body will be made ready for them to see (bathed, dressed, hair combed, makeup applied).
* What the **coffin** is, and what it looks like: "A special box that holds the body, made of wood, with handles and a lid. The inside looks a bit like a bed with a pillow."
* What the children will see in the viewing room.
* They can touch the person or the coffin if they want to.
* They can draw a picture or put things in the coffin.

Parents may need to share their own understanding of life, death and faith. Clergy will usually be able to help with this.

16

The funeral

It is helpful to explain the reason for the funeral:

  * "We all join together with family and friends in order to
    remember the person who died."
  * "To surround them with our love and say goodbye."
  * "To celebrate the person's life."

Children need to know **who** will be there, **what** will happen, **where** the
service will take place and **when** and **why** they are doing things:
Where the funeral service will be held (crematorium, church, at the
grave-side) and that it may include hymns, scripture readings, a short
sermon, prayers for the person who has died, and **eulogies** (speeches)
about the person's life.

Children need to anticipate seeing others expressing a wide variety of
feelings, including laughter as well as tears, and let them know that any
and all of these feelings are okay

That after the service, everyone will gather at the family home or some
other location to share memories, laugh and cry with others who knew
the special person

When a child doesn't want to attend

It's been said that families who love together grieve together. Parents
should be encouraged to invite children to go to the funeral or memorial
service. If a child absolutely refuses to go they shouldn't be forced but
ensure the child isn't made to feel guilty for not attending. Let the child
know that you are available to talk about it whenever they are ready.

Ideas to Help Children
Say Goodbye (continued)

When a child doesn't want to attend you could:
* Take pictures and make them available whenever the child wants to see them.
* Make a video or tape recording of the proceedings.
* Write an account of the service: who was there, what happened, who said what.

If parents are too upset to support their children at the funeral

The parent needs to tell the children exactly how they are feeling and explain that they can count on someone else to be there for them in addition to themselves.

It is good to make contingency plans. A family member or close friend who knows the children can be asked to sit with them and care for children as needed. Someone could sit behind or near the end of their row, so they can leave the service unobtrusively and go outside with the children if they become too restless.

Ideas for explaining Burial

The coffin is taken to the cemetery in a **hearse** (a special car that carries the coffin with the dead body).

Everyone follows in a **funeral procession** (a quiet parade of cars) to the **cemetery** (where dead people are buried).

Everyone gathers around the **grave** (a special hole that's already been dug in the ground) and words and prayers are spoken. Sometimes the coffin is lowered into the grave and family members will gently throw handfuls of dirt or flowers on top.

Later a **grave stone** (a stone or marker) is placed at the grave to mark the place where the body is buried: It tells --------- name, birthday, date of death, and maybe a special saying or poem of loving memory. Later when we visit the cemetery, we can go to the grave to remember and feel close to ---------, because the love we have for each other continues to live on, even after our special person has died.

Ideas for explaining Cremation

Cremation takes place in a special building called a **crematorium**. In this building is a room with a special fire – not like any room in our house, and not like the fire in our fireplace.

Because --------- is dead, they will not feel anything at all during cremation. A body without life cannot feel heat or pain.

This special fire is very, very hot – hot enough to burn the body and turn it into very fine, very soft ash.

What is left of a dead body is called **ashes**. The ashes may be put into a small container called an **urn**. The urn may be buried in the ground or placed in a special building, or the ashes may be scattered in a beautiful place, such as in the sea or in a garden.

19

Helping families with funerals

Where's
Molly Now?
A handbook for
Childhood Bereavement

Assisting with the funeral

This is a painful period for the family when confusion and shock reign within the bereaved family and important decisions must be made. Clergy can encourage family members to be together and to participate in planning the service. Single parents, separated and divorced families may face additional problems. Remember that all children, regardless of age, will be deeply affected by the death and it is essential to ensure that they will feel included at this crucial time.

After the funeral

Many families have reported that, while their clergy were helpful at the time of the funeral service, they needed more support afterwards. The funeral takes less than an hour but the grieving becomes part of that individual's or family's life. Clergy often try to remain close to the family or see that a network of support is established. The family may be unable to reach out on their own.

While coping with the funeral calls for one expression of ministry, supporting the long term grief process requires another.

How a bereaved family's faith in God may be affected

After the death of a loved one each family member reacts to God differently. Anger may be directed at a "God of retribution", or they may feel that God has forsaken them.

When a child has died it may be especially difficult to understand "why" or "for what purpose", or hard to accept that God would take back a child.

Faith may be shaken. A spiritual leader can help by offering support at this time. It can become a time of examining faith in oneself and in God. How this question of faith is handled can be critical to the future faith of the individual who is being supported.

Take the time to be a true friend and seek the wisdom to counsel gently. Remember that listening to another's pain is the most helpful way to assist the grieving process.

Resist the temptation to provide pat answers!

Other resources that are available

The wisest helpers are often those who know when to make a referral. In addition to your own ministry, children's bereavement support groups can provide very effective support. (See page 36)

Individual differences are important to remember

The family may appear to be coping rather well at the time of the death and the funeral. In actual fact they are more likely to be in shock, feeling nothing but a sense of numbness.

As time goes on, grief may manifest itself in tears, depression, anger and physical symptoms of distress. Panic and guilt are often present. Along with depression, many may feel hostility and resentment.

No one follows a prescribed "grief pattern".

Eventually, families begin to resume normal activities and even to see hope returning to their lives. It is unreasonable to expect the bereaved to "become themselves" again after such grief. The death of someone close profoundly and permanently changes a family and its members.

How a Bereavement Affects family Dynamics

When someone dies the family unit undergoes permanent changes. Children rely on adults for cues for what the appropriate response should be following a death. The way that parents function and respond to the changes after the death of a family member will have a strong influence on children's reactions and how they reconstruct their lives. A child's response to death and loss must be viewed in the context of their family.

Parents

* When parents are dealing with their own grief responses they often have a difficult time supporting their child emotionally.
* Parents may find it more difficult to discipline their children and set clear boundaries; this confuses children and makes them feel more insecure.
* Some parents do not acknowledge that their children are experiencing any grief problems and say that the children seem to be fine and they don't need any help.
* Some parents will cope with a traumatic death by avoiding all reminders of the death and then find it difficult to talk to their children. This often happens following suicide or murder. If the death is not talked about openly children receive the message that they are not supposed to talk about the death within the family unit. This is sometimes referred to as the "conspiracy of silence".
* Children are more likely to be at risk of complications if the family environment was chaotic or unstable before the death.
* Parents may need to share their own understanding of life, death and faith. Clergy will usually be able to help with this.

Death of a Sibling

* Initial support for the family often focuses on helping the grieving parent.
* Siblings may worry about their own safety and possible death.
* Younger siblings sometimes have an extremely difficult time when they reach the age at which their sibling died.
* Older siblings may be plagued with guilt for not "looking out" for their younger brother or sister.
* Some children attempt to take over the identity of the deceased child in order to ease their parents' grief.
* If the relationship was difficult they may fantasise that they caused their sibling's death, (that the good child died and the bad one survived).
* If parents idealise the dead sibling the surviving child can feel jealous, angry, and devalued.

Death of a Parent

* Children will naturally worry about who will care for them.
* They may believe that the parent died because the parent didn't love them.
* Children who survive a suicide or murder of a parent are more likely to experience persistently low self-esteem.
* Children may blame the remaining parent for the death. They may idealise the dead parent and become quite hostile to the surviving parent.

The Death of a Baby or Child

How clergy and pastoral workers can help

How you communicate with and support parents at the time of a death can profoundly affect their experience of the loss of their child, and may influence how they support their other children.

As there are often traumatic circumstances surrounding the death of a baby or child it is important to give the parents and children time to talk about their worries and anxieties.

Parents and children need:

* To be encouraged to spend time with the baby both before and after the death, in private and appropriate surroundings.
* Parents need to be reassured that inviting the child to be involved in such things as viewing the body, planning the funeral and other activities can often be helpful at the time and will assist with the grieving process in the future.
* Signposting to other organisations will enable them to meet with other parents who have experienced the death of a baby.

There are several reasons why children may have difficulties grieving:

* They may have little or no memories of their dead sibling therefore it is difficult for them to accept the reality of the loss.
* Their sibling may have had a long and complicated illness, and they may have been separated for some time. Here there may be guilt around a sense of relief.
* Children may have found their sibling dead and witnessed the resuscitation.

Suggestions for a Baby's Funeral

Some suggestions to consider

* Ask families what they would like to have happen during their child's service.
* Offer a variety of ideas and alternatives for the funeral to help families make an informed decision that they will not later regret.
* Families may want something tangible to hold on to remember their baby such as a cuddly teddy bear to hug.
* Suggest creating a memory box that includes various keepsakes such as hand and footprint Kits, a baby's quilt and a beaded bracelet with child's name.

Some suggestions for a baby's funeral

* A cradle or Moses basket for baby to rest in during the service
* Display of flowers that represent the child's birth/death month
* Symbolic remembrance items for guests such as packets of 'Forget-Me-Not' flower seeds to plant in honour of the grieving family's baby
* Video of service
* Photography of family with their infant
* Music that may be symbolic of their child
* Readings of poems and letters written for the child by the family
* Light memorial candles

Ideas for Supporting families

Early Days

Acknowledge the death through visits, phone calls, sympathy cards and flowers.

Let the family know how sad you are about the death and the pain they must be feeling. If you knew the person who died, talk about your memories and their special qualities.

Give special consideration to children at the funeral and in the months to come (they may need extra attention that grieving parents are unable to give).

If the death was sudden they may need your help to inform their children, family and friends.

You may offer to answer the phone and help with children's practical needs.

Offer specific help such as running errands, completing forms, feeding and walking pets and watering plants.

Help to transport children to school, birthday parties, or extra-curricular activities.

Encourage the bereaved to express their feelings of grief. Give them time to talk about their loss, as much and as often as they want to.

Call often. When you call ask, "How are you doing today?"

The bereaved family may not always return phone calls right away. However, they will feel comforted by your efforts even if you only leave a message.

Talk in your natural tone of voice. Listen.

Later On

Offer specific help:
- "I'm going to the shops. What do you need?"
- "Can I look after your children this afternoon?"
- "I will bring dinner round for the family."
- "I can take your child to ballet lessons."
- "Shall I come and baby-sit to give you a break?"
- "Do you want to get out tonight to talk, walk, or both?"

Remember important days such as birthdays, the death anniversary, Mother's Day, Father's Day, and any other significant day, which may be difficult for the bereaved. A telephone call, visit, or card means a great deal to the bereaved.

Be aware that bereaved parents whose child has died can sometimes find it difficult to be around children of a similar age.

Locate local support through church groups, bereavement organizations. Give the information to the bereaved family.

Help families understand that they need to be patient and not to expect too much of themselves.

The bereaved family will continue to need support well beyond the acute mourning period, even for years.

Recognise that grieving has no time limit and varies from person to person, both in the way they express their grief and the time required to stabilise.

Ideas for Supporting families (continued)

Helpful considerations:

It won't help to avoid mentioning the loss or the person's name out of fear of reminding them of their pain (they haven't forgotten it!)

Be careful not to change the subject when they mention their loved one.

Bereaved people don't need to be forced to talk about their loss; they will when the time is right.

Try not tell the bereaved what they should feel or do as this can be very annoying.

Steer clear of making any comments which in any way suggest that their loss was their fault.

If a child has died you may exacerbate the parent's anger if you say that at least they have their other children (children are not interchangeable; they can not replace each other). Grief over the loss of one child does not discount the parents' love and appreciation of their living children.

You may lose their confidence if you say that you know how they feel (unless you've experienced their loss yourself you probably don't know how they feel).

Don't be afraid to cry or laugh in front of the bereaved. Or assume that when a grieving person is laughing, they are over anything or grieving any less.

Don't wait until you know the perfect thing to say. Just say whatever
is in your heart or say nothing at all. Sometimes just being there is
comfort enough.

Remember the overlooked mourners (grandparents, uncles, aunts, close
friends etc.) who need your support too.

Never underestimate the impact of grief on children.

Children understand and retain a lot more than they may show.

Think before saying any of the following:
- It was God's will.
- It was meant to be.
- He's in a better place now.
- Time heals all wounds.
- I know just how you feel.
- You are still young enough to have more children.
- Are you not over it yet?
- At least you have other children.
- Your child is in a better place.
- It was for the best.
- Now you will have an angel in heaven.
- It could have been worse...

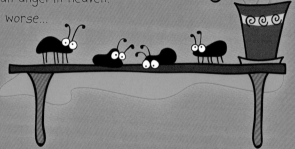

Guidelines for Responding to Bereaved Children

* If you are approached by a bereaved child wishing to talk about their experiences, be careful not to change the subject.
* If you are not free to talk immediately, make a definite time to talk with the child.
* Listen to the child. If necessary seek the help of a trained counsellor.
* Don't minimise the loss that the child has suffered.
* Reassure the child that grief and tears are a natural response of which they should not be embarrassed or ashamed.
* Do ask them what support would help them.
* Suggest a place where the child can go if they are upset or just need space in the church buildings.
* Don't be afraid to ask for help from others if you are unsure how to cope with a particular issue.
* Avoid the use of euphemisms such as 'passed away', 'falling asleep', 'lost', or 'taken by Jesus.'
* It is best to be honest and avoid misleading or confusing the child. If you are unsure about anything, say that you don't know but will try to find out.
* Make a note of important dates and acknowledge anniversaries, such as the first after the death, birthdays and special occasions such as Mothers Day and Christmas.
* The length of the grieving process shouldn't be underestimated. You will need to keep a special watch on the child throughout the next few years.

When Children Might Need More Help

Where's
Molly Now?
A handbook for
Childhood Bereavement

Children exhibit signs of loss and grief in many ways but feelings of sadness and loss usually lessen over time. It is a combination of prolonged changes in behaviour, intensity of feelings and actions that signal onward referral may be needed.

Red Flags to Identify Children who need onward referral
Indicators of Complex Grief

* Difficulty talking about the deceased
* Uncontainable aggression
* Symptoms of anxiety, shown by a refusal to go to school and extreme clinging to the surviving parent
* Sleep difficulties and/or nightmares after a year
* Changes in eating patterns
* Marked long-term social withdrawal
* School difficulties or a serious decline in academic performance, continuing after nine months
* Persistent self-blame or guilt (Indicative of clinical depression)
* Self-destructive behaviour or desire to die: in this case, a child should be offered individual support immediately regardless of how long ago the death occurred.

Worden W (1996)

Engaging with other faiths

As Christians today we cannot isolate ourselves from those of other faiths. Each church and congregation will have its own links with the leaders of other faith groups in the local community. Respect for the religious and cultural mourning rituals of other faiths will encourage you to seek their wisdom and advice when necessary.

You may wish to compile your own useful directory of contacts or get in touch with your diocesan adviser or representative for liaising with other faith leaders.

Appendices

Where's
Molly Now?
A handbook for
Childhood Bereavement

Bibliography

Astley, J & Francis, L (1992) Christian Perspectives on Faith Development: Gracewing

Beckwith, I (2004) Postmodern Children's Ministry: Zondervan.

Bowlby, J. (1980) Attachment and Loss: Harper Collins. New York.

Coles, R. (1990) The Spiritual Life of Children: Houghton Mifflin.

Dyregrov, A. (1992) Grief in Children: Jessica Kingsley Publishers.

LeShan, EJ. (1987) When a Parent Is Very Sick. Macmillan.

Fowler, J. (1981) Stages of Faith: Harper Collins. New York.

Grollman EA. (1990) Talking about death: Beacon Press, Boston

Worden JW. (1996) Children and Grief: The Guildford Press. New York.

Wass H. Corr CA (1984) Childhood and Death: Hemisphere Publishing Corp.

Recommended Reading

Beyond the Rough Rocks Winston's Wish
ISBN: 978-0953912339
Offers practical advice for families in the immediate days and weeks when suicide has been the cause of death

Dear Grandma Bunny Brunna D
ISBN: 978-1-4052190-1-3
A wonderfully simple explanation for young children about death, funerals and feelings.

Muddles Puddles & Sunshine Winston's Wish
ISBN: 978-1869890582
Helpful series of activities and exercises to help children remember the person who has died and express their feelings

Remember Me Penhaligon's Friends
ISBN: 978-0-950757-0-4
Guidance for schools/educational settings when dealing with childhood loss, bereavement and critical incidents.

Remember Me Always Penhaligon's Friends
ISBN: 978-0-9550757-3-5
Handbook to help bereaved families care for grieving children.

Remember Me Too Penhaligon's Friends
ISBN: 978-0-9550757-1-1
Handbook for healthcare professionals.

Samantha June's Missing Smile Kaplow J & Pincus D
ISBN: 978-1591478096
A story about coping with the loss of a parent.

Straight Talk about Death for Teenagers Grollman E
ISBN: 978-0807025017
Teenagers express their feelings through poems and talk of their own experiences.

Help for the Hard Times Hipp E
ISBN: 978-1568380858
Exploration of various losses that teenagers may be facing in their
lives. Written in the appropriate language and well illustrated for this age-group.

Josh Jeffs S & Thomas J
ISBN: 978-1841014234
Coming to terms with the death of a friend.

Mudge, Gill and Steve Dainty J
ISBN: 978-0715148877
The story covers the questions children tend to ask: Why God allows children (and
others) to die; what a funeral is and what happens after death?

Rosie Jeffs S & Thomas J
ISBN: 978-1841014227
Coming to terms with the death of a sibling.

Waterbugs and Dragonflies Stickney D
ISBN: 978-0829816242 0
This children's book explains the Christian belief of life after death through a story about
the lifecycle of waterbugs and dragonflies.

We Were Gonna have a Baby We Had An Angel Instead Schweibert P
ISBN: 978-0972424110
A book to help very young children cope with the death of a sibling before birth, at birth
or shortly after birth.

What on Earth Do You Do When Someone Dies? Romain T
ISBN: 978-1-57542-055-4
In simple, honest words describes the strong, confusing feelings triggered by death and
suggest ways to feel better.

When a Friend Dies Grootman ME
ISBN: 978-1575421704
Speaks directly and simply to anyone who has suffered the loss of a friend, particularly
teenagers.

When Someone Very Special Has Died Heegard M
ISBN: 978-0962050206
A practical format for children to understand the concepts of death and develop coping
skills for life. Children, with supervision, illustrate & personalise their loss through art.

Where's
Molly Now?
A handbook for
Childhood Bereavement

Where to Get Help

The organisations listed below offer specialist support and some have interactive websites that are designed especially for bereaved young people.

Childhood Bereavement Network

A national network working with bereaved children and young people, their families and caregivers, that offers an online directory of services available nationally.

www.childhoodbereavementnetwork.org.uk

Childline

National helpline for children with any kind of problem or difficulty.
www.childline.co.uk

CRUSE

Bereavement care for adults.
www.crusebereavementcare.org.uk

Merry Widow

A website for anyone who has lost a partner. There are helpful survival guides and a message board to share thoughts and feelings.
www.merrywidow.me.uk

Papyrus

A website to help young people who may be suicidal.
www.papyrus-uk.org

Parentline Plus
A very helpful parenting website with lots of useful links.
www.parentlineplus.org.uk

RD4U
Website especially for young people, interactive, managed by CRUSE.
www.rd4u.org.uk

Rip Rap
A website for those whose relatives have cancer. www.rip.rap.org.uk

Survivors of Bereavement by Suicide
www.sobs.admin.care4free.net

The Compassionate Friends
Organisation to support parents who have lost a child of any age.
www.tcf.org.uk

The Way Foundation
Organisation to support young widows.
www.wayfoundation.org.uk

Also helpful - To stop unwanted direct mail to those who have died.
www.the-bereavement-register.org.uk

Notes